REDUCE, REUSE, RECYCLE!

Water

Jen Green

PowerKiDS
press.

New York

Published in 2010 by The Rosen Publishing Group Inc.
29 East 21st Street, New York, NY 10010

Copyright © 2010 Wayland/The Rosen
Publishing Group, Inc.

First Edition

Editor: Katie Powell
Designer: Elaine Wilkinson
Illustrator: Ian Thompson
Consultant: Kate Ruttle
Picture Researcher: Shelley Noronha
Photographer: Andy Crawford

Library of Congress Cataloging-in-Publication Data

Green, Jen.
    Water / Jen Green.
        p. cm. -- (Reduce, reuse, recycle!)
    Includes index.
    ISBN 978-1-61532-235-0 (library binding)
    ISBN 978-1-61532-246-6 (paperback)
    ISBN 978-1-61532-247-3 (6-pack)
    1. Recycling industry--Juvenile literature. 2. Water--Juvenile literature. I. Title.
    HD9975.A2G74 2010
    333.91'16--dc22

                                    2009023729

Photographs:
Cover: UpperCut Images/Getty Images. 1 Image Source/Getty Images, 2 Wayland Picture Library, 4 NASA, 5 Ecoscene /
photog, 7 Stone+ / Getty Images, 8 Image Source/Getty Images, 9 Jim Nicholson / Alamy,10 ImageShop/Corbis
Corporation/ImagePick, 11 © Steven Gillis/LOOP IMAGES/Getty images, 12 Wayland Picture Library, 13 Peter Cade/Getty
Images, 14 ISTOCK, 15 Wayland Picture Library,16 Stockbyte/Photolibrary.com, 17 ISTOCK, 18 © Jennie Woodcock/
Reflections/Corbis, 19 Wayland Picture Library, 20 © Jennie Woodcock/Reflections/Getty Images, 21 UpperCut Images/Getty
Images, 22 © Fabio Cardoso/Corbis, 23 Kraig Scarbinsky/Getty Images, 24 Stockbyte/Photolibrary.com, 25 © Heide
Benser/zefa/Corbis, 26 © MM Productions/Corbis, 27 Recycle Now, 28 t Stockbyte/photolibrary.com, 28 b, 29 t, c, b Wayland
Picture LibraryWith thanks to RecycleNow.

The author and publisher would like to thank the following models: Lawrence Do of Scotts Park Primary School,
Sam Mears, and Madhvi Paul.

Manufactured in China
CPSIA Compliance Information: Batch #WAW0102PK: For Further Information
contact Rosen Publishing, New York, New York at 1-800-237-9932

Contents

Words in **bold** can be found in the glossary.

Watery planet

Earth looks blue from space, because it is mostly covered by seas and oceans.

Fresh water is important for life. Most of the Earth's surface is covered with water, but nearly all of that is salty seawater, which would make you sick if you tried to drink it. Less than three percent of Earth's water is fresh, and most of that is ice.

Water has three forms: liquid water, invisible **moisture** in the air called **water vapor**, and ice, which is **frozen** water.

Did You Know?

Plants, animals, and people all need water, but people often waste it. We can help save water by following the 3 R's—**reduce**, **reuse, and recycle**. Reducing means using less of something. Reusing is when something is used again, for example, when kitchen water is reused in the yard. Recycling is when water is cleaned so it can be used again.

◄ *All animals, such as these zebra, need water to survive.*

Circling water

The water on our planet is always moving, circling between the land, sea, and air. This is called the **water cycle**. As the sun warms the sea, water rises into the air as water vapor. This is called **evaporation**. The moisture turns into tiny water **droplets**, which gather to make clouds.

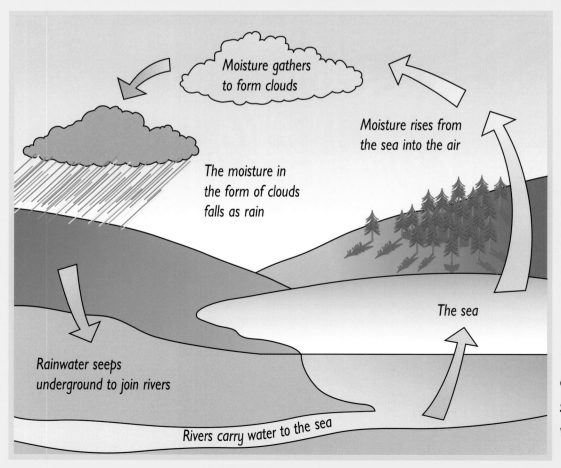

Moisture gathers to form clouds

Moisture rises from the sea into the air

The moisture in the form of clouds falls as rain

Rainwater seeps underground to join rivers

The sea

Rivers carry water to the sea

◀ This diagram shows the water cycle.

When clouds shed rain, plants and trees soak up water. The rest trickles into the ground or into lakes and rivers. Rivers return water to the sea to complete the water cycle. This natural recycling has gone on for millions of years.

▼ *Water evaporates from lakes in the sunshine.*

7

Water for life

No one can go for more than a few days without water. We take in water by drinking and by eating, since food contains a lot of water. Tomatoes and melons are made up of nearly all water!

▶ *You need to drink a lot of water when you exercise.*

You need to replace the water you lose. We lose water as we exercise, through sweat, as we breathe out, and when we go to the bathroom.

▼ On a cold day, the moisture you breathe out turns back into tiny water droplets that you can see.

Did You Know?

About 65 percent of your body is made up of water.

Water and work

Water has hundreds of uses. Farmers use huge amounts of it to look after their animals and water their crops. Water flowing in rivers provides drinking water. People usually dam the river to save water. The lake that forms behind the dam is called a **reservoir**.

◄ A cow has to drink 4 quarts of water to produce 1 quart of milk.

Factories use water for washing, cooling, and making everything from soft drink cans to newspapers. It takes at least 8 gallons (30 liters) of water to make a newspaper, and 26 gallons (100 liters) to make one can that holds a small amount of soda!

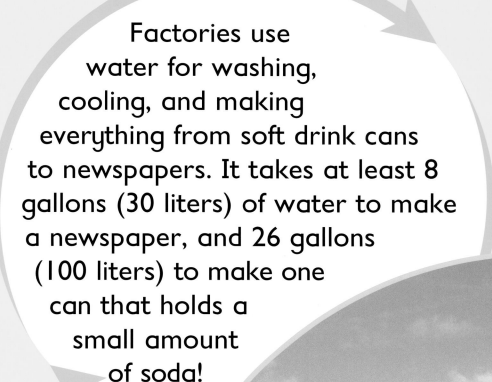

▶ Reservoirs supply cities with the water they need.

Reduce, reuse, recycle

The amount of water in the world has stayed about the same for millions of years, but the number of people on Earth is growing and they need more water. It is important to use water carefully, so there is enough for everyone and everything that needs it.

▶ *A dripping faucet can waste a quart (liter) of water an hour—that adds up to a bathtubful a week!*

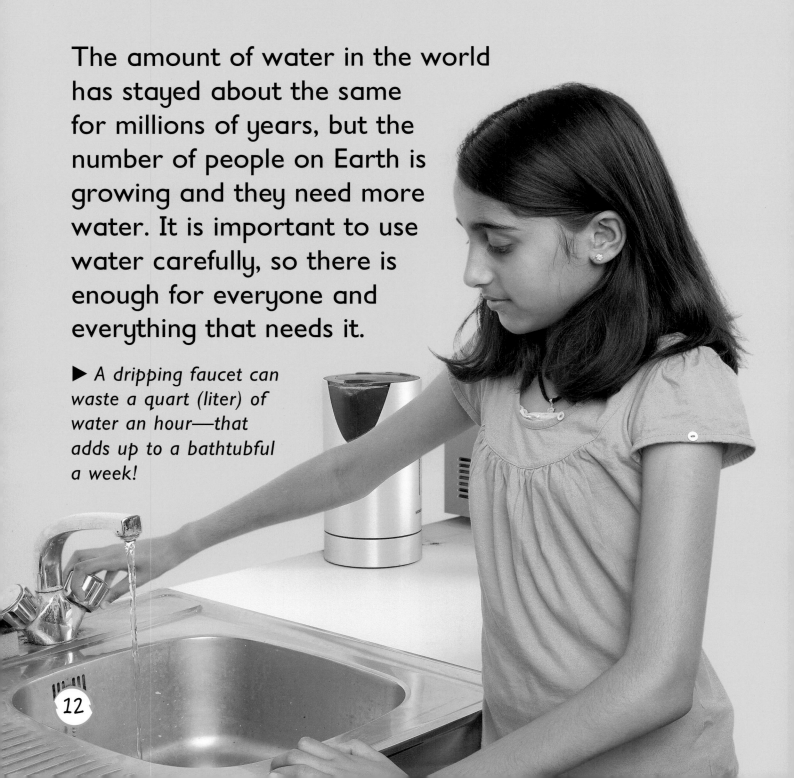

▶ Use a sink of water to wash your hands instead of running the faucet.

You Can Help!

Dripping faucets waste water. Make sure you turn faucets off completely.

There are many ways you can reuse and recycle water. You can also reduce the amount of water you use. For example, do not run the faucet while you brush your teeth and don't flush the toilet more than necessary.

Sharing water

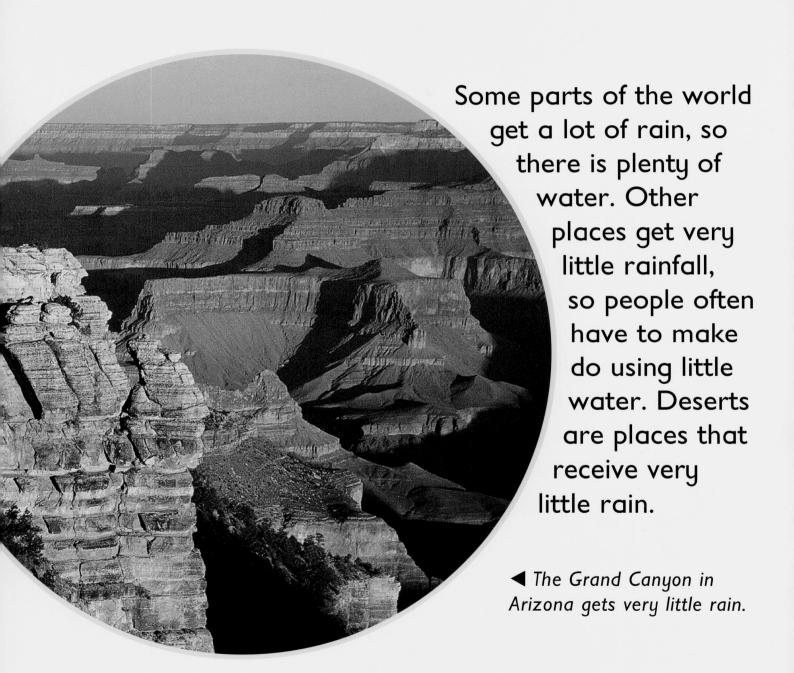

Some parts of the world get a lot of rain, so there is plenty of water. Other places get very little rainfall, so people often have to make do using little water. Deserts are places that receive very little rain.

◀ The Grand Canyon in Arizona gets very little rain.

The wettest town in the U.S.A. is Quillayute, Washington, which receives 104 inches (264 centimeters) of rain a year. The driest town is Yuma, Arizona, with just 2.6 inches (6.6 centimeters) a year.

MEASURING RAINFALL

1. Make a rain gauge to measure rainfall by cutting a plastic bottle in half. Ask an adult to help you do this. Put the top half upside-down inside the bottom half to make a funnel.

2. Tape a ruler to the side.

3. Dig a small hole outside for the rain gauge to sit in, so it does not fall over.

▲ Take readings once a week, and empty the rain gauge. Add the weekly totals each month. Make a chart to record rainfall throughout the year.

Water on tap

The water we use comes from rivers, lakes, and reservoirs. In some countries, such as the United States, the water is cleaned and then pumped into our homes. Water flows out of the faucet whenever we need it. In other countries, people often have to share one faucet, or walk a long way to fetch water.

▲ *This young girl has walked for more than an hour to get water and will have to carry it home in heavy containers.*

In Europe, people use 80 gallons (300 liters) of water a day. That is enough to fill two bathtubs! In the U.S.A., people use more—about 132 gallons (500 liters). In poor countries, with little water, people use less than 13 gallons (50 liters) a day.

In rich countries, we use a huge amount of water every day. Cleaning and pumping water is expensive and uses **energy**. In poor countries, people get by with much less water. Wherever you live, it is important to use water carefully.

▼ Using a car wash wastes a lot of water.

How do we use water?

Think about all the ways you use water at home and at school. Families and schools use water for washing, drinking, cooking, and cleaning. Taking a shower, brushing your teeth, and filling a pot all use water. The central heating system that keeps you warm may also contain water.

▼ *Bathtubs and washing machines use a lot of water.*

WATER USE CHART

1. Make a chart to record water use at home on one weekend.

2. List all the ways your family uses water under headings such as, "Brushing teeth," "Washing dishes," "Using toilet."

3. Ask family members to check a column each time they use water.

4. Use the chart to work out how much water your family uses in two days.

▼ This boy is starting to make his own "water use chart."

Did You Know?

• Brushing your teeth or washing your face and hands uses 1.3 gallons (5 liters) water

• Flushing the toilet uses 2.6 gallons (10 liters)

• A five-minute shower uses 8 gallons (30 liters)

• A full bathtub uses 32 gallons (120 liters)

• Washing dishes by hand uses 1.3–2.6 gallons (5–10 liters)

• A dishwasher uses 12 gallons (45 liters)

Water for washing

A lot of the water we use is for washing. We use water to clean our bodies and our clothes. We also use water to clean bikes and cars outdoors. You can reduce the amount of water you use and still keep clean!

▼ *Turn the faucet off while you brush your teeth. This will save water.*

SAVING WASHING WATER

1. Take a quick shower instead of taking a bath.

2. Put the plug in before you wash your hands and face, do not use running water.

3. Ask an adult to make sure the washing machine is full before it is used. That way, your family will do fewer wash loads.

▶ *Use a bucket of water to wash the car, instead of a hose or a car wash.*

In the kitchen

In the kitchen, we use water for all kinds of everyday things. We use water to make hot drinks, wash and cook food, and clean up afterward. There are lots of ways to save water in the kitchen. If everyone saved just a little, it would add up to a huge amount.

▼ Water used for rinsing plates can be reused in the yard.

▶ Dishwashers use a lot more water than washing dishes by hand.

SAVING KITCHEN WATER

1. Rinse dirty plates and glasses in a sink of water, not under a running faucet.

2. Wash fruit and vegetables in a sink of water, too.

3. Ask an adult to wait until the dishwasher is full before using it. Then you will run fewer washes.

Down the drain

The water that goes down the drain contains **sewage**, and also soap, **bleach**, and other cleaning products. It has to be cleaned before it flows back into streams and rivers, but cleaning water is expensive. We should try to reduce the amount of dirty water that flows down the drain in the first place.

▲ Sewage contains harmful **germs** that can cause **disease** and make people and animals sick.

REDUCING WATER

1. Ask an adult to place a plastic bottle full of water in the **cistern** tank of your toilet. The bottle takes up space in the cistern, so less water is used with every flush.

2. Do not use more soap than you need when washing your hands.

3. Do not play in water sprinklers because it wastes water.

▶ *Playing in water sprinklers is a lot of fun, but it wastes a lot of water.*

In the yard

We use lots of water in the yard, particularly if we water plants with a sprinkler. A sprinkler can use as much water in an hour as a whole family uses in a day! Using a watering can instead reduces the amount of water used outdoors.

◀ Plants in flower beds need less water than plants in pots and hanging baskets.

▼ Buy a **rain barrel** to save rainwater. Fill your watering can from the barrel.

You Can Help!

If you water the yard in hot, sunny weather, most of the moisture disappears before plants have a chance to soak it up. Water in the evening instead.

SAVING WATER IN THE YARD

1. Save water from washing fruit and vegetables, and rinsing dishes, to water the garden.

2. Ask your parents to think about buying plants that do not mind dry **conditions**, such as rock roses, heather, and lavender.

3. Put **compost** on flower beds to reduce evaporation. That way plants will need less water.

27

Make a water filter

At a **water treatment plant**, water is cleaned by being filtered through sand and gravel. Make your own water filter to see how this works.

1. Put a filter paper in the funnel and stand the funnel in a jar.

2. Mix a little soil with water in another jar. Empty the dirty water into the funnel. Look to see how clean the water is.

WARNING
The filtered water may look clear, but it's not really clean, so don't drink it.

3. Put a new filter in the funnel. Add a handful of sand and gravel. Pour more dirty water into the funnel. Repeat step 2.

4. The water should be cleaner this time.

Further Information and Web Sites

Topic map

HISTORY

The ancient Egyptians were among the first people to channel water into fields. Find out more about the ancient Egyptians by using a library or the Internet.

GEOGRAPHY

The water that gushes from the faucet comes from local rivers, lakes, and reservoirs. Look at a local map to find out where there are rivers, lakes, and reservoirs in your local area.

MATH

Look back at your water use chart (page 19). Divide the total for two days by two and multiply by 365 to find out how much water you use in a year.

ENGLISH

Write a story or poem about the water cycle, perhaps from the point of view of a water droplet.

ART/DESIGN

Design a poster explaining why we should all use water carefully and try to reduce, reuse, and recycle!

RELIGIOUS STUDIES

Water is used in religious ceremonies by Christians, Muslims, Hindus, and other faiths. Can you find out how and why water is used in these religions?

Further reading

Good for Me: Water by Sally Hewitt (PowerKids Press, 2008)

How The Water Cycle Works by Jen Green (PowerKids Press, 2008)

Saving Water by Jen Green (Gareth Stevens Publishing, 2005)

Web Sites

Due to the changing nature of Internet links, PowerKids Press has developed an online list of Web sites related to the subject of this book. This site is updated regularly. Please use this link to access this list: http://www.powerkidslinks.com/reduce/water/

Glossary

bleach a powerful cleaning product

cistern the small tank above the toilet that holds water for flushing

compost natural materials that rot to make fertilizer for the yard

condition the state something is in

disease an illness

droplet a tiny drop

energy the power to do work

evaporation when water changes from a liquid into a gas

fresh water water that is not salty

frozen when water is cold, it turns into ice

germ a tiny living thing that can make you sick

moisture wetness

rain barrel a large container used to store rainwater outdoors

recycle when water is cleaned for reuse

reduce to make something smaller or use less of it

reservoir a man-made lake used to store water

reuse when something is used again

sewage dirty water from homes, containing chemicals and human waste

water cycle the constant movement of water around Earth

water treatment plan a place where water is cleaned so it is safe to drink

water vapor moisture in the form of a gas

Index

Numbers in **bold** refer to a photograph.